W9-BFG-128

Simple Experiments with

Levers

Chris Oxlade

WINDMILL
BOOKS
New York

Published in 2014 by Windmill Books, An Imprint of Rosen Publishing
29 East 21st Street, New York, NY 10010

Produced for Windmill by Calcium Creative Ltd
Editors for Calcium Creative Ltd: Sarah Eason and Jennifer Sanderson
Designer: Emma DeBanks

Photo Credits: Cover: Shutterstock: Amadorgs. Inside: Emma DeBanks: 9,
10, 11; Dreamstime: Alexander Morozov 7, Bugtiger 23, John Alphonse 25,
Landd09 5, Le-thuy Do 29, Paul Prescott 8, Rene Van Den Berg 28, Sergey
Gorodenskiy 1, 22, Sergey Yakovlev 14, Shuiyanxii 21, Vasilijs Shilovs 24;
Shutterstock: Abel Tumik 4, AISPIX by Image Source 13, Corepics VOF 16,
Fidel 15, Ixpert 20, James Steidl 17, Pryzmat 12, Pukach 6; Tudor Photography:
18, 19, 26, 27.

Library of Congress Cataloging-in-Publication Data

Oxlade, Chris.
Simple experiments with levers / by Chris Oxlade.
pages cm. — (Science experiments with simple machines)
Includes index.
ISBN 978-1-61533-756-9 (library binding) — ISBN 978-1-61533-829-0 (pbk.) —
ISBN 978-1-61533-830-6 (6-pack)
1. Levers—Experiments—Juvenile literature. 2. Force and energy—
Experiments—Juvenile literature. I. Title.
TJ147.O885 2014
621.8—dc23
2013004410

Manufactured in the United States of America

CPSIA Compliance Information: Batch #BS13WM: For Further Information contact Windmill Books, New York, New York at 1-866-478-0556

38179000743490
Apple 10/14

Contents

Simple Machines

What do you think of when you hear the word "machine?" Perhaps you imagine an aircraft, a backhoe, or even a computer. Machines are things that make our lives easier by helping us do jobs. Aircraft, backhoes, and computers are complicated machines, made up of thousands of parts. However, many machines are very simple. They have only one or two parts. The **lever** is one type of simple machine.

Types of Simple Machine

There are six types of simple machine. Levers are one. The others are the **wheel and axle**, **pulley**, **screw**, **wedge**, and **inclined plane**. Some of these machines do not really look like machines. Some do not have any moving parts. However, they still help us do jobs in our everyday lives.

A pair of scissors is just one of many everyday objects that use levers.

These levers are helping to cut through tough branches.

What Is a Lever?

A lever is a bar or rod that **pivots**, or moves, on a fixed point called a **fulcrum**. Whenever you play on a seesaw, use a pair of scissors, or dig with a spade, a lever is helping you. In this book, you will find plenty of examples of levers at work. There are also some interesting experiments for you to do. Try them out and discover for yourself how levers work.

Parts of a Lever

A lever is a very simple machine. In its simplest form, it is just a long bar. However, it must be a very strong bar, to prevent it from bending when you push or pull on it. A lever is normally quite thick and made from a tough material, such as metal or wood.

Special Levers

Some levers are made for a specific job. Examples include the metal crowbars that builders use and the handles on a pair of scissors. We can use all sorts of things as levers, as long as they are the right shape and strong enough. For example, we can use the blade of a screwdriver or a thick branch as a lever.

Screwdriver blades are very useful for levering open some lids, such as those on paint cans.

A seesaw is a simple lever. The fulcrum is at the center.

The Fulcrum

A lever always needs a fulcrum on which to pivot somewhere along its length. When you push or pull on part of a lever, the lever pivots around the fulcrum. Different kinds of levers have fulcrums in different positions.

Pushes and Pulls

In this book, you will see the words "**force**," "**effort**," and "**load**." A force is a push or a pull. Simple machines change the direction or **magnitude** of forces. An effort is a force that you make on a simple machine. The load is the **weight** or other force that a machine moves.

7

Levers in Action

Now that you know what a lever is, we can take a look at some levers in action. We will look at how they work, what pushes and pulls are needed to work them, and what pushes and pulls levers make.

Up and Down

When one end of a seesaw goes down, the other end goes up. Imagine a friend sitting at one end of a seesaw. You could push down on the other end of the seesaw to lift up your friend. This works because a seesaw is a lever. The push you make is the effort on the lever. The load is your friend's weight. The fulcrum is in the middle. The lever allows your effort to overcome the load. Remember that the load is always the force that you are trying to overcome with the lever.

You can lift a friend off the ground by using a seesaw as a lever.

This sailor is using a lever to steer his boat.

Steering a Boat

Sailors steer some small sailboats with a rudder, which is joined to the back of the boat by hinges. When the rudder turns to one side, it pushes on the water, which makes the boat turn. The sailor turns the rudder from side to side with a long handle called a tiller, which is a lever. The effort is the sailor's push or pull on the tiller. The load is the push of the water on the side of the rudder.

Seesaw Levers

Here is an experiment you can try on the seesaw in your local playground. A seesaw is a big lever, with its fulcrum in the middle. Investigate levers by using one.

1 Sit on one end of the seesaw, and have your friend sit on the other end. Move backward and forward slightly until the seesaw balances. Can you see how the seesaw works as a lever?

You Will Need:

- A seesaw
- A friend

2 Move closer to the fulcrum, and ask your friend to stay still. What happens?

3 Climb off the seesaw. Ask your friend to stay on it, and to move close to the fulcrum. Push down on the other end of the seesaw with your hands to lift up your friend. How much effort did you need?

So Simple!

When the seesaw was balanced, your weight pushed down at one end and balanced your friend's weight at the other end. When you moved closer to the fulcrum, your weight had less effect, so your friend's weight lifted you up. That was also why you could lift your friend with your arms.

Making Forces Larger

Levers are often used to make forces larger. A lever can make the effort you put in (the push or pull you make on the lever) into a much greater force. This force overcomes the load on the lever. Sometimes levers make forces many, many times larger.

Levers for Builders

A crowbar is a builder's tool that is designed to be used as a lever. When a crowbar is being used for lifting a floorboard, for example, the short end is pushed under the edge of the floorboard, and the builder pushes down on the long end. The fulcrum is where the curved part of the bar presses on the floor. The load is the weight of the floorboard and the resistance of the nails keeping the floorboard down. A hammer works in the same way when it is used to pull out a nail.

This crowbar is being used to pull a nail out of a piece of wood.

Effort

Pulling back and down on a spade handle lifts the soil.

Effort

Increasing the Effort

The lever increases the effort that the builder supplies. This is because the point where he pushes down on the lever is farther from the fulcrum than the place where the lever pushes up on the floorboard.

Levers for Digging

A garden spade can work as a lever for digging soil. You push the blade into the soil, then you pull backward and downward on the handle. The spade pivots around the bottom of the handle, and the blade forces the soil upward and forward.

13

Cutting and Gripping

Many simple tools that we use for cutting and gripping things in the kitchen, in the garden, and around the house, are made from levers. Most are made from two levers that work together. The point at which the levers are joined is the fulcrum for both levers.

Scissors and Other Cutters

The handles and blades of pairs of scissors and garden shears are levers. Pressing the handles together makes the blades move past each other, cutting through materials. Cutting near the fulcrum works best for tough materials because the levers increase your effort. Bolt cutters cut through tough metal. They have long handles. The long handles make your effort much bigger, which helps to overcome the resistance of the tough metal.

Placing a branch near the fulcrum of a pair of garden shears makes the effort you supply much greater.

A pair of pliers is a simple machine made of two levers.

Gripping Levers

Levers can help us to grip things much more tightly than we could with our fingers alone. A pair of pliers is made up of two levers, like a pair of scissors. Pressing the handles together squeezes the object between the jaws.

Kitchen Tools

Kitchens are a good place to find levers at work. Some can openers use levers. Pressing the handles together forces the cutting disks through the lid of the can, and also grips the can tightly. Another sort of simple machine, the wheel and axle, helps you to cut around the lid.

First-Class Levers

In most of the examples of levers we have looked at so far, you push or pull on one end of the lever, the load is at the other end of the lever, and the fulcrum is somewhere in between. Scientists call levers such as these **first-class levers**. Here are some more examples of first-class levers.

Lifting and Moving

A simple lever, such as a crowbar, a long metal pole, or even a strong branch from a tree, can be used as a first-class lever to lift and move heavy objects, such as boulders, paving stones, or large logs. All that is needed is somewhere to rest the lever to make a fulcrum. This could be a brick or a small log.

A rower uses oars as levers to pull the boat through water.

The weight of the concrete block stops the crane from toppling over.

Rowing with Levers

You can use an oar as a first-class lever. The fulcrum is where the oar is attached to the boat. The effort is the pull that the rower makes on the oar, and the load is the resistance of the water at the other end of the oar.

Staying Steady

A counterweight is a weight that helps something balance, to stop it from toppling over. In a crane, the weight of the object being lifted up is balanced by a concrete block on the other side of the crane. The arm of the crane works as a lever.

The Power of Levers

Try this experiment to discover how levers can make forces much bigger. It will show you how it is possible for you to lift or move a heavy object with a small pull or push.

1 Put some books into your box. The box should be quite heavy, but light enough for you to lift up one side of it with your hand.

2 Put the box on the floor, and put a wooden block about 1 foot (30 cm) from it. Slide the end of the broom handle under the edge of the box, and rest it on the block. Push down on the other end of the handle to lift up the edge of the box. How much effort did it take?

18

3 Try pushing down on the handle at a position nearer to the wooden block. Do you have to use more or less effort this time?

So Simple!

You may have noticed that it was much easier to lift the box by using the broom handle as a lever than it was by hand. When you pushed at the end of the lever, the lever increased the force you made. When you pushed closer to the fulcrum (the block), you had to use more effort.

19

Levers in the Past

Nobody knows when the lever was invented, but it must have been thousands of years ago. We do know that the ancient Greeks and Romans used levers for all sorts of jobs. Before people had complicated machines to lift and move things, they used simple machines such as levers.

Moving the Earth

The famous Greek mathematician Archimedes, who lived more than 2,200 years ago was one of the first people to understand how levers make forces larger. Stories say that he claimed, "Give me a place to stand and a lever long enough, and I will move the whole world!"

Archimedes said that he could move an object as big as Earth with a lever!

This is a shaduf. It is used for lifting water from one field to another.

Lever-Powered Weapons

The Greeks and Romans put levers to work in construction machines and weapons of war. They made huge catapults with lever arms that threw rocks and burning tar at their enemies. The effort to move the lever arm was made by a huge counterweight or by tightly twisted rope.

Lifting Water

A shaduf is an ancient machine for lifting water to water crops. It has a long lever arm that is lifted high off the ground. At one end of the arm is a weight, and at the other is a bucket for water. The weight of the water is the load, and the weight of the rock is the effort. In some parts of the world, people still use shadufs.

Moving the Fulcrum

Some levers have the fulcrum at one end instead of in the middle. A **second-class lever** has the fulcrum at one end, the load in the middle, and the effort applied from the other end. Just like a first-class lever, it still makes the effort bigger.

Crushing Levers

You can often see second-class levers in a kitchen. Garlic presses, nutcrackers, and can crushers are all machines that use second-class levers. The fulcrums are at one end, you press at the other end, and the object being crushed is in between. The object is normally close to the fulcrum, because this increases your effort as much as possible. In the garlic press and nutcracker, there are two levers joined at their fulcrums.

Can you see where the fulcrum is in this nutcracker?

22

The lever in a wheelbarrow includes everything from the wheel to the handles.

Opening with Levers

A bottle opener is also a second-class lever. Pulling up on the end of the handle makes it easier to lift the edge of the bottle cap.

Wheeling Loads

Can you see a lever at work in a wheelbarrow? In fact, the whole wheelbarrow is a second-class lever. The wheel is the fulcrum. The load is the weight of the objects in the barrow. The effort is the upward pull that you make on the handles.

23

Making Forces Smaller

All the levers we have looked at so far make forces larger because they increase the effort you make. Some levers make forces smaller instead. The fulcrum is still at one end, as with a nutcracker. However, in these levers the load is at the opposite end from the fulcrum, and the effort is in the middle. A lever arranged like this is called a **third-class lever**.

Gently Does It

A pair of tweezers is a pair of third-class levers. Their fulcrums are at the end, where the arms join. You press halfway along the tweezers to grip things with the tips of the arms. The tweezers make your effort smaller, so that you can pick up delicate objects without squashing them. Chopsticks work in the same way.

Tweezers make your press smaller so that you do not crush delicate objects. Can you see the fulcrum?

Your lower arm is one of the levers in your body. You move it with your biceps.

Levers in Your Body

Did you know that your lower arm is a third-class lever? You use it as a lever to lift up things. Your elbow joint is the fulcrum. It is moved by an effort from muscle, which attaches your upper arm to your lower arm bones close to the elbow. The load is the weight of whatever your are lifting. Your jaws are levers, too! Can you guess where the fulcrum and the muscles that make the effort to open and close your jaws are?

25

More Types of Lever

In this experiment you can see how putting the fulcrum at the end of a lever allows it do different jobs.

You Will Need:

- Two short rulers
- Small rubber bands
- A pencil
- Modeling clay

1 Put two rulers together, one on top of the other. Put two rubber bands around the rulers near one end, around ¼ inch (6 mm) apart, to keep them together. Slide a pencil between the two rulers and between the rubber bands to make a fulcrum.

2 Hold the rulers at the opposite end from the fulcrum, and put a small piece of modeling clay between the rulers, about halfway along them. Squeeze the rulers together and watch what happens to the modeling clay.

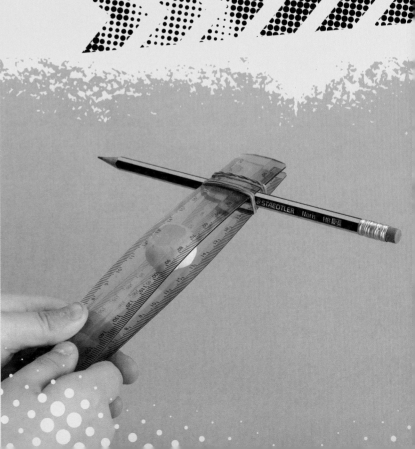

3 Hold the rulers near the fulcrum and put the modeling clay between the rulers at the opposite end. Try to squash the modeling clay. Is it easier or more difficult than before?

So Simple!

Holding the rulers at the end made your effort greater, so it was easy to squash the modeling clay. It created a second-class lever. Holding the rulers near the fulcrum made your push smaller, so it was harder to squash the modeling clay. It formed a third-class lever.

Amazing Machines

Levers are very handy simple machines. Many levers make our lives easier by increasing the effort we make. They let us lift and move objects that are too heavy to move by hand. They make gripping things tightly, cutting through materials, and squashing tough objects easier. Other levers help us handle delicate objects.

What Did You Learn?

Have you tried the simple experiments in the book? What did you learn about levers?

In Big Machines

Levers are useful even just on their own. However, we also find them in more complicated machines. Many machines with moving parts have levers working away inside. These complex machines include cars, in which levers help to steer, airplanes, in which levers move parts of the wings and landing gear, and backhoes, in which levers make up the digging arms.

A backhoe has levers that move and tip its bucket.

Can't Live Without Them

Humans have been using levers for thousands of years. Levers might be simple, but it would be almost impossible for us to live without them. There are probably more of them around than you think! There are levers in the kitchen, in tool boxes, and in office equipment such as paper cutters and staplers. Keep an eye out for levers wherever you go!

Even your bicycle has levers that you use for braking.

Glossary

effort (EH-fert) The amount of force applied to an object.

first-class levers (FURST-KLAS LEH-vurz) Levers in which the fulcrum is between the load and the effort.

force (FORS) A push or a pull.

fulcrum (FUL-krum) The point on which a lever turns.

inclined plane (in-KLYND-PLAYN) A slope used as a simple machine.

lever (LEH-vur) A rod or bar that moves around a point called a fulcrum.

load (LOHD) The push or pull that a lever overcomes, which may be the weight of an object.

magnitude (MAG-nih-tood) The measurement of something's strength.

pivots (PIH-vutz) Moves, spins, or turns on a point.

pulley (PU-lee) A wheel with a rope around it that works as a simple machine.

screw (SKROO) A simple machine with an inclined plane wrapped around a cyclinder.

second-class lever (SEH-kund-KLAS LEH-vur) A lever in which the fulcrum is at one end, the effort is at the other end, and the load is in between them.

third-class lever (THURD-KLAS LEHvur) A lever in which the fulcrum is at one end, the load is at the other end, and the effort is in between them.

wedge (WEJ) A triangular object used as a simple machine.

weight (WAYT) The force of gravity on an object, which pulls the object downward.

wheel and axle (WEEL AND AK-sul) A simple machine made up of a disk with a fixed bar running through its center.

Read More

To learn more about levers, check out these interesting books:

Dahl, Michael. *Scoop, Seesaw, and Raise: A Book About Levers.* Amazing Science: Simple Machines. Mankato, MN: Picture Window Books, 2006.

Gosman, Gillian. *Levers in Action.* Simple Machines at Work. New York: PowerKids Press, 2010.

Howse, Jennifer. *Levers.* Science Matters. New York: Weigl Publishers, 2009.

Volpe, Karen. *Get to Know Levers.* Get to Know Simple Machines. New York: Crabtree Publishing Company, 2009.

Yasuda, Anita. *Explore Simple Machines!* Explore Your World. White River Junction, VT: Nomad Press, 2011.

Websites

For web resources related to the subject of this book, go to: www.windmillbooks.com/weblinks and select this book's title.

Index